RAOUL WALLENBERG

by Michael Nicholson
and David Winner

B
Wallenberg

T12007

For a free color catalog describing Gareth Stevens' list of high-quality children's books call 1-800-341-3569

Picture Credits

Ben Uri Collection, p. 12 (above); Bildarchiv Preussischer Kulturbesitz, p. 19; W. C. Burgard, pp. 4, 48, 54; Camera Press, pp. 23, 24, 38, 40, 42, 50 (above); Ghetto Fighters' House, Israel, p. 26; Martin Gilbert, p. 25; Agnes Havor-Takach, pp. 12 (below, both), 27, 37 (below), 55 (below); Imperial War Museum, p. 14 (below); Janina Jaworska, Warsaw, p. 18; Jethro Films, Australia, p. 55 (above); Keystone Collection, pp. 8, 29, 50 (below); Kulturgeschichtliches Museum, Osnarruck, p. 16; Nina Lagergren, pp. 6, 7 (top left, below), 8; Michael Nicholson, pp. 53, 56, 57 (above); Polish Military Museum, Chicago, p. 20; Popperfoto, pp. 21, 30 (below), 43; Raoul Wallenberg Foundation, Sweden, pp. 7 (top right), 33 (all), 44, 45; Svenskt Pressfoto, p. 57 (below); Statens Konstmuseer, Stockholm, p. 59; Tom Veres, p. 47; Weimar Archive, pp. 30 (top), 35; Weiner Library, p. 13.

Cover painting by Borin Van Loon

The authors would like to thank the following for their kind help and advice: George Stern, Dr. Odon Zinger (Chief Rabbi, Budapest), Mrs. Seiffert, Mrs. Lujza Havas, Gyorgy Krasso, Professor Schweitzer (Rabbinical Seminary, Budapest), Dr. Istvan Szondy, and Stephen Ward.

The publishers would like to thank especially Nina Lagergren and all the people at the Raoul Wallenberg Foundation in Stockholm for their invaluable assistance in providing information and photographs. The publishers would also like to thank Martin Gilbert for his kind permission to reproduce a map from his book, *Atlas of the Holocaust*, and Mr. W. C. Burgard of Ann Arbor, Michigan, for permission to reproduce his paintings originally made for the University of Michigan *Michigan Alumnus* (May 1985).

North American edition first published in 1989 by
Gareth Stevens Children's Books
RiverCenter Building, Suite 201
1555 North RiverCenter Drive
Milwaukee, Wisconsin 53212, USA

Library of Congress Cataloging-in-Publication Data

Nicholson, Michael, 1937-
    Raoul Wallenberg.
    (People who have helped the world)
    "First published in the United Kingdom in 1988 with an original text by Exley Publications Ltd. and Gareth Stevens Inc."—Verso t.p.
    Includes index.
    Summary: Traces the life of the diplomat who saved Hungarian Jews during World War II and mysteriously disappeared after the Russians occupied Budapest.
    1. Wallenberg, Raoul—Juvenile literature. 2. World War, 1939-1945—Civilian relief—Hungary—Juvenile literature. 3. Jews—Hungary—History—20th century—Juvenile literature. 4. Holocaust, Jewish (1939-1945)—Hungary—Juvenile literature. 5. Diplomats—Sweden—Biography—Juvenile literature. 6. Righteous Gentiles in the Holocaust—Biography—Juvenile literature. 7. Hungary—History—1918-1945—Juvenile literature. [1. Wallenberg, Raoul. 2. Jews—Hungary. 3. Holocaust, Jewish (1939-1945)—Hungary. 4. Diplomats] I. Winner, David, 1956- . II. Title. III. Series.
    D809.S8W3265 1989 940.54'779439'0924 [B] [92]   88-2078
    ISBN 1-55532-845-8
    ISBN 1-55532-820-2 (lib. bdg.)

Series conceived and edited by Helen Exley
Picture research: Kate Duffy and Margaret Montgomery
Research: Diana Briscoe
Editorial: Margaret Montgomery
Series editor, U.S.: Rhoda Irene Sherwood
Editor, U.S.: Rita Reitci
Editorial assistant, U.S.: Scott Enk
Additional end matter, U.S.: Ric Hawthorne

Printed in Spain

2 3 4 5 6 7 8 9 96 95 94 93 92 91 90

RAOUL WALLENBERG

*The Swedish diplomat who
saved 100,000 Jews from the Nazi Holocaust
before mysteriously disappearing*

**by Michael Nicholson
and David Winner**

Gareth Stevens Publishing
Milwaukee

RAOUL G. WALLENBERG

An impossible mission

In the darkest days of July 1944, an obscure young Swedish diplomat abandoned the comfort and safety of home for an impossible rescue mission in one of the most dangerous places on earth.

His name was Raoul Wallenberg. His destination: Nazi-controlled Hungary.

The Nazis there planned to murder every one of the country's 750 thousand Jewish men, women, and children. Wallenberg's brave ambition was to rescue as many as possible from the jaws of death.

The plan to kill Hungary's Jews was the last part of the so-called "Final Solution," the Nazi dictator Adolf Hitler's attempt to kill every single Jew in Europe.

By 1944, Hitler had largely succeeded. The pitiless and all-powerful Nazis had scoured the continent looking for Jews to kill. Millions were already dead. Whole Jewish populations had been destroyed. Now the Nazis and their many thousands of eager accomplices were determined to repeat the process in Hungary — with the last surviving major Jewish community in Nazi-occupied Europe.

Raoul Wallenberg had been sent by his government, but he was armed with little more than courage and his extraordinary personality. In his battered luggage were a diplomatic passport, an old revolver, a bundle of money, and a secret list of names. As he went south by train through Nazi Germany itself and on to the Hungarian capital of Budapest, Wallenberg's task seemed hopeless.

The thundering train was carrying him into history. Yet until that fateful journey, there was little to suggest that Raoul Wallenberg would become a hero.

"Who was this Wallenberg, the mention of whose name was enough to stir life into the half dead? He was not a diplomat — his was merely a title of convenience. He was a son of neutral Sweden, product of a family of privilege and position. Why, then, had this young man chosen to stride into the . . . nightmare of Budapest, 1944?"
Kati Marton,
from Wallenberg

"The greatest unsung hero of World War II"
BBC-TV's
"Man Alive"

Opposite: W. C. Burgard's symbolic illustration of Raoul Wallenberg, a young man who faced the Nazis alone.

5

Raoul's mother, Maj Wallenberg, was a beautiful and determined woman.

A privileged childhood

Raoul Wallenberg was born on August 4, 1912, into one of Sweden's greatest and most privileged families. The Wallenbergs were famous diplomats and bankers and were on excellent terms with the Swedish royal family.

Raoul never knew his father, an officer in the Swedish Navy who died of cancer three months before Raoul was born. But his beautiful and determined mother, Maj, and his grandmother showered him with love and attention. When he was six, his mother remarried and Raoul soon had a brother and a sister.

Raoul was a sensitive, happy, loving child, who was good at his schoolwork. He enjoyed hiking and swimming but did not care for competitive sports. He was good at drawing, and he made all the posters for the events at his school. Raoul was greatly interested in airplanes and ships — he knew all of the battleships of World War I. Construction drew his attention, and from an early age he was visiting building sites all over Stockholm. He enjoyed talking to the men working there, from the bricklayers to the engineers. Aware of Wallenberg business interests, Raoul began collecting and reading company reports, asking questions until he understood the information. Often he imagined how he would run these companies.

Raoul's grandfather, Gustav Wallenberg, a famous diplomat, took charge of Raoul's education. Gustav was a portly Victorian figure who dressed in starched stand-up collars and rough tweeds. He loved to tell Raoul stories about his own grandfather, a famous banker, and his great-grandfather, a bishop. Raoul enjoyed these stories about his forefathers, whom he used to call the "big men."

Gustav was determined that his grandson should have a broad, cultured approach to life and that he should learn many languages. A summer in Germany and a year in France helped him master German and French. Through his studies, he also became fluent in English and Russian. After he left school, he joined the Swedish army to fulfill his compulsory military service. Upon his discharge, he was ready to begin his university studies.

"Born into the distinguished Wallenberg family, the 'Rockefellers of Scandinavia,' which for generations had produced diplomats, bankers, bishops, shipping and industrial magnates, Raoul Wallenberg was expected to succeed and make a name for himself — family tradition demanded this of him."
Lilian E. Stafford,
from Michigan Alumnus,
May 1985

Detta kort skall för att äga gillighet ovill-korligen vara försett med innehavarens fotografi.

Raoul Wallenberg was born into a family of great wealth and power. He was a much-loved child.

Top left: Raoul at the age of three with his grandfather, Gustav Wallenberg.

Above: Pictured at the age of eleven on his first passport, when he traveled alone to visit his grandfather in Turkey.

Left: Raoul as a schoolboy at the age of twelve.

7

Raoul loved the United States, especially its openness, democratic freedom, and mobility. During his student days in the U.S., he enjoyed hitchhiking and considered it to be great practice in the arts of diplomacy and negotiation. This picture was taken by one of his friends on the Hudson Bridge in New York.

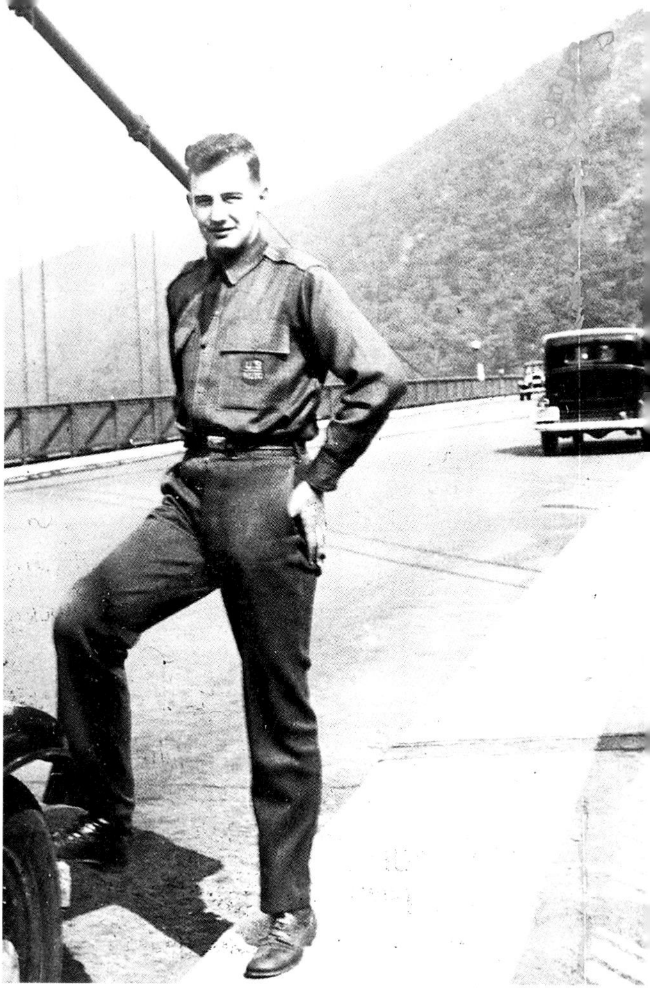

"Wallenberg seemed as American as could be — in his dress, his manners, and the slang expressions he quickly picked up. Everyone called him 'Rudy.'"

Clarence Rosa, classmate at the University of Michigan

" . . . a very talented person, with lots of ideas, who learned very easily. Once, when Wallenberg had his arm in a sling, he made all his projects with his left arm, and his presentations were excellent."

Richard Robinson, Raoul's classmate at the University of Michigan

A student in the United States

Gustav wanted Raoul to become a banker. But Raoul was much more interested in architecture, so he was sent to the United States to study that subject. He proved to be a brilliant, hardworking student. Out of his class of 1,100 people, he won the medal given each year to the top student. Yet he was modest and had a great sense of humor. He often mimicked pompous speechmakers and imitated animals. No one suspected he came from a famous family.

Wallenberg loved the United States. He liked its relaxed, freewheeling atmosphere. Like so many of his countrymen before him, he blossomed there. For several generations, like many immigrants from other

countries, Swedes have crossed the Atlantic to build new lives in the United States. Originally, they landed at Delaware Bay, and later they formed important communities in Minnesota, with other communities in New York and on the western seaboard. Raoul marveled at the prosperity they had achieved.

Raoul loved the challenge of hitchhiking. "I went three hundred miles on fifty cents," he wrote to his grandfather. But the best part of hitchhiking, he wrote, "is the great practice it offers in the art of diplomacy and negotiating. You have to be on your guard. And it brings you into intimate contact with so many different kinds of people." This proved only too true. Returning from the World's Fair with his summer earnings, Raoul was robbed by four men who had offered him a lift. They seized his money and shoved him into a ditch. But as he later wrote, "Strange, but I did not feel any fear the whole time. It was more like an adventure."

Both his absence of fear and the capacity for self-detachment that he showed then would one day prove important for thousands of people.

He was also fun to be with. One summer, he traveled to Mexico with a friend to stay with an aunt and uncle. Years later, his young cousin Birgitte recalled his visit: "I adored him. . . . He was wonderful with me, playing with me and trying to teach me chess. He was so unlike most grown-ups; he actually took notice of me, a lonely only child. . . . It was always fun being with Raoul."

After his studies, Raoul went to Cape Town in South Africa to gain experience in commerce and banking. In 1936, at his grandfather's suggestion, he moved to Haifa, in what was then Palestine, to work at the Holland Bank. Raoul did not really think he was suited for such work, and he wrote to his grandfather, "I am not cut out for banking. . . . A banker should have something of the judge in his makeup and a cold, calm, calculating outlook. . . . I think I have the character for positive action, rather than to sit at a desk and say No to people."

A year later his grandfather died, and Raoul was at last free to choose his own career. Unfortunately, he could not become an architect back home because his

"We didn't know he came from such an important, wealthy family; he never talked about that. While he was here he had to budget his money. It had to cover tuition, books, room, and meals. That was part of the training his family had in mind for him."
Julia Senstius,
teacher at Michigan State
Normal College

9

training in the U.S. was not recognized in Sweden.

Through family connections, he found work with a Jewish refugee, Koloman Lauer, who ran an import-export business dealing in exotic food. Raoul's job was to travel around Europe using his knowledge of languages and immense personal charm to buy and sell foods. The job took him to Germany and Hungary. Within eight months he became a director.

While still in Haifa in modern-day Israel, Raoul met several Jews who had come there in order to escape oppression in Germany. Raoul listened as his new friends told of their experiences.

Hitler and his "master race"

Meanwhile, in Germany, events had been unfolding which were to change not only Raoul's life but the course of the whole world.

In the early 1930s a dictator, Adolf Hitler, preaching a hate-filled new creed, Nazism, had seized power in Germany. Hitler believed that certain types of people were biologically superior to others. According to this idea, Jews, Slavs, black people, and all non-Europeans were deemed to be *untermenschen* (subhumans). Germans and other "Aryans," especially people with blond hair and blue eyes, were the so-called "master race."

Hitler despised different types of people — communists, homosexuals, intellectuals, gypsies, people with physical and mental disabilities, and many others. But he had a special hatred for Jews, whom he imagined to be the source of all Germany's problems.

Hitler blamed the Jews for Germany's defeat in World War I, for communism, for Germany's economic troubles, and for the catastrophically high unemployment that hit the country in the 1920s and early 1930s. He even hated Christianity because he thought it was "tainted" by its Jewish origins!

Adolf Hitler was enormously popular with the millions of Germans who voted his political party into power in 1933. Germany had been beaten in World War I and humiliated in the years after the war. Also, the abrupt postwar change from a monarchy to a republic gave rise to political confusion. Rapidly rising

inflation made money nearly worthless. Finally, widespread unemployment made things even worse.

Hitler promised to make Germany a proud and powerful nation again. He promised to restore the value of money. He promised jobs for the country's six million unemployed people. Overwhelmed with problems, the Germans were willing to follow any strong leader who offered them simple solutions.

Adolf Hitler was certainly a strong, charismatic leader and a persuasive speaker. When he said that the Jews were the source of all Germany's troubles, the people responded to him.

Hitler's vicious anti-Jewish propaganda also struck a chord with his followers because anti-Semitism — as hatred of Jews is called — was not a new idea. It had long been a particularly vicious form of racism, and it had also been a sinister undercurrent in European civilization for many centuries.

A history of persecution

The problem started soon after Christianity was born about two thousand years ago among a small group of Jewish followers of Jesus, who was himself a Jew.

Adolf Hitler was voted into power in Germany in 1933. Many Germans saw him as a "strong leader." He imagined that the Jews were a manifestation of cosmic evil that threatened not only Germany but the whole planet. He dreamed of waging war against them and creating a "racially pure" Aryan empire to rule the world.

In the years following the death of Jesus, a rivalry developed between the new religion, Christianity, and the older religion of the Jews, Judaism. Later, Christianity triumphed in some areas and became the state religion of mighty Imperial Rome. But in its triumph, the Christian church turned against the Jews.

Some of the early popes branded the Jews as "Christ-killers," a myth that persists to this day in many backward parts of the Christian world. It was widely believed in eastern Europe before and during the Nazi terror. Because the Jews did not believe Jesus was the Messiah, some church leaders also declared that the Jews must be "in league with the devil."

For many centuries this sort of Christian teaching of contempt for Jews was widely accepted. The most outlandish anti-Jewish fantasies were believed. In the superstitious Middle Ages, Jews were regularly accused of bizarre and impossible crimes, from poisoning Christian wells to killing Christian children in order to drink their blood!

Jews were persecuted for generation after generation. The rulers of some European countries expelled them or forced them to live in separate areas, called ghettos, away from Christians. Jews had to wear distinctive badges and were forbidden to own land.

Whenever a natural disaster occurred, such as an outbreak of plague, it was often the Jews who got the blame, and angry Christian mobs would take "revenge" by butchering the local Jewish community.

But even during the worst times of anti-Jewish persecution, it was always accepted that Jews were human beings and that they had souls. The aim of the Christian persecutors was not to kill Jews but to convert them to Christianity.

The Jews, then, had faced generations of persecution, cruelty, and oppression in Europe. Down the centuries, they had often been massacred and used as scapegoats for other people's problems.

During the nineteenth century, life improved considerably for the Jews as modern, emancipated Europe came into being. Jews became active in the cultural life and professions of nearly every country. And they could participate freely in politics. But anti-Semitism had not gone away; it had only changed its shape.

"Mankind loves to hate. It makes us feel good and right.... We need scapegoats ... so that we can project our own anger and hostility."
Professor Ron Baker, survivor of the Holocaust

Despite centuries of persecution, Jewish life and culture had survived and flourished in Europe, especially in eastern Europe.

Opposite, top: A happy Jewish family. Many Jewish people in Europe were highly successful. They felt secure and they certainly had no idea of the coming horror.

Opposite, left: The magnificent synagogue in Budapest, outside and inside views. It would be one of the few synagogues in Europe to survive World War II.

Fekete árnyék!

Both before and during the Holocaust, Jews were the targets of vicious Nazi propaganda. Above: This Hungarian Nazi poster portrays a gross caricature of a Jew as a "black shadow" over Hungary. Below: The Nazis often depicted Jews as "corrupting" blond Aryan women.

The Nazi onslaught

Nothing in the Jews' long and painful history had prepared them for the intensity and scale of the anti-Semitic Nazi onslaught that faced them from the moment Hitler seized power in Germany in 1933.

In the years before 1933, Jews had been beaten up in the streets by gangs of Nazi supporters. Now, the terror increased a hundredfold. Synagogues and Jewish cemeteries were attacked and desecrated by the thousands. Rabbis were beaten up in public. Jewish shops and businesses were boycotted. Brown-shirted Nazi thugs daubed Jewish shops with anti-Semitic slogans.

Jews were banned from the universities, the arts, and the professions. But that was just the beginning. Soon many Jews were being murdered at random. Slogans declaring that Jews were "not wanted" appeared on shops, restaurants, and street signs. Nazi newspapers declared that "The Jews are our misfortune." The so-called "racially inferior" Jews were deprived of their rights. They were terrorized and hounded out of their homes in towns and villages across Germany.

In 1935, the Nazis passed the notorious Nuremberg Laws. Jews, many of whom had served their country bravely in World War I, were now stripped of their citizenship. Marriages or sex between Jews and "Aryans" was strictly forbidden. Later, Jewish property was "Aryanized" — in other words, stolen.

The horror spreads

Within a few years the Nazi terror began to spread. Hitler made plans to add more territory to the Third Reich, as he called his government. Again the Jews were the first to suffer. In some neighboring countries, local Nazi political parties began their own persecution of Jewish citizens.

In 1938, Hitler took over Austria, the country where he had been born, in the infamous event known as the *Anschluss*. Austrian Nazis took to the streets in the capital, Vienna. "They came up like rats from the sewers," remembered one terrified Jewish girl who survived. Overnight, the once-civilized city of Vienna became a city of anti-Semitic terror as Nazi gangs roamed the streets searching for Jews to beat up and humiliate. Within a month, over five hundred despairing Jews had killed themselves.

In November 1938, the Nazis went on a rampage of destruction that became known as *Kristallnacht* — the "night of broken glass." Jewish shops and homes throughout the Reich were looted and burned. The Jews were physically attacked and some were killed. Afterward, laughing crowds jeered as Jewish men and women were forced to scrub the streets. Later, the Nazi government ordered the Jews to pay a heavy fine for the destruction of their own property!

The Jews are trapped

Confronted by systematic terror, the Jews tried to flee.

But at this fateful moment, the world began to close its doors to the Jews. In 1938, many of the world's leading nations met for a conference at Evian in France to consider the problem of the thousands of Jews who were trying to escape the Nazi terror.

Throughout this period, with few noble exceptions like the government of the tiny Dominican Republic, most countries said they had no room to take more than a handful of Jews. Enormous, underpopulated Australia declared that it did not have a "racial problem" and did not want to import one.

The United States said it had no room for more than a few thousand Jews. Britain's answer was the same. The British also severely restricted the number of Jews who could go to Palestine, which Britain controlled at the time. Britain did not care to upset the local Arab population, which didn't want the Jews either.

The Jews were trapped in Europe.

World War II

Meanwhile, Hitler had been dreaming of conquering Europe and building a German "new order" on the continent, based on his racial theories. In his insane scheme, Poland and the Soviet Union would become part of the German Reich, and the Slavic peoples would become the Nazis' slaves. The Reich, declared Hitler, would last a thousand years.

By 1939, Hitler's armies were the strongest in the

Nazi anti-Semitism drew heavily on prejudices such as the idea that all Jews were rich.

This Nazi cartoon showed Jews as manipulators of financial institutions in the U.S. At the same time, the Nazis also portrayed Jews as manipulators of world communism in the Soviet Union!

Ein Vorschlag zur Ordensfrage

Der „Adler der Republik" in zwei Klassen: gold und silber. Die goldene Ausgabe nur für „überzeugte Republikaner", am roten Band zu tragen; die silberne Ausgabe für „auf dem Bob der Tatsachen stehende Republikaner", am schwarz-rot-gelben Band zu tragen.

During the Second World War, anti-Jewish terror was instigated all over Nazi-occupied Europe. Jews were rounded up, concentrated in ghettos, and forced to wear yellow stars on their clothing. But mass cruelty and segregation were merely the first steps in the Nazi plan to murder every Jew in Europe.

world. Now he used them to invade Poland. World War II had begun.

Europe was plunged into the most cruel and destructive war in its often bloody history. In the years that followed, Hitler's armies conquered France, Belgium, Holland, Norway, Denmark, Yugoslavia, Greece, and most of eastern Europe. They held sway over most of the rest of the continent.

Under the cover of the chaos of war, Hitler planned another, quite separate war against the isolated and defenseless Jewish people of Europe.

Mass murder

In June 1941, Hitler attacked the Soviet Union. During the invasion, the Germans soon overwhelmed the Soviet troops facing them.

Just behind the fast-advancing tank columns, special killing squads called *Einsatzgruppen* were sent to slaughter every Jew they could find among the occupied land's civilian population.

In a few months the entire Jewish population of

hundreds of villages and towns was systematically and ruthlessly massacred.

In some places the Nazis were helped by local militia and police. In one case, the Germans even set up chairs and benches for the local population to come and watch the killing.

Many centuries of Jewish history, learning, and culture in these countries came to a brutal and sudden end. About 1.5 million Jewish men, women, and children were murdered in just a few months.

In most places there were no survivors. The inhabitants of whole towns were lined up and shot. The slaughter was so thorough that not even the names of all the victims will ever be known.

But these mass shootings were considered "messy" and inefficient by the Nazis. And they wasted ammunition needed for the war. A new and more monstrous policy was soon to be devised.

The "Final Solution"

On January 20, 1942. a committee of top Nazi officials gathered in a house in the Berlin suburb of Wannsee to draw up a more efficient plan for a "Final Solution" of the so-called "Jewish question" in Europe. Every single Jew in Europe, they decided, was to be put to death without exception.

The Nazi bureaucrats included the infamous Adolf Eichmann, whom Raoul Wallenberg would meet two years later in Hungary. They decreed that Jews would be rounded up wherever they lived throughout Europe and sent by train to specially built, new extermination camps in Poland.

A new, more "efficient" method of mass slaughter had been devised — death by poison gas.

New extermination complexes were built in remote spots in the Polish countryside at Chelmno, Sobibor, Belzec, Lublin-Majdanek, Treblinka, and Auschwitz-Birkenau. They were equipped with gas chambers capable of killing hundreds, sometimes thousands, of people at a time.

The sole purpose of these camps was to eliminate millions of innocent living human beings — men, women, and children of all ages — people from every

"When the officer inquired whether after the war people would not ask what had happened to the millions of Jews, Eichmann replied: 'A hundred dead is a catastrophe. A million dead is a statistic.'"

A witness at the Nuremburg war crimes trials

"Wallenberg said that even he did not believe some of the atrocities until he himself was an eyewitness. He went over to a brick factory where they had over ten thousand Jews herded together into an area so small that they were forced to stand up closely packed together for five days, old people and young children alike, without any sanitary facilities. He saw them himself standing there, and also being loaded into box-cars, after which the doors were nailed shut. He said many died, just standing in the brick factory."

Iver Olsen,
War Refugee Board
representative in Stockholm

country in Europe. All by-products would be used to help the German war effort. All clothes, jewelry, gold tooth fillings, and even long hair for wigs would be carefully salvaged.

These death camps would carry on their foul work uninterrupted for three years. By the time they finished, a total of six million Jews would be murdered, and with them much of a unique culture.

The gas chambers

Although Winston Churchill, the British prime minister during World War II, called this destruction of the Jewish people "a crime without a name," it is today known as the Holocaust. Another term for it is "Shoah," the Hebrew word for annihilation.

The Nazi extermination plan could not have worked if the Jews had known what lay in store. Nothing in their experience or history had prepared them for systematic mass execution of *everybody*. And at every stage of the destruction process, the Nazis played upon their victims' hopes.

When they were put on death trains, the Jews were told they were being "resettled" in the East.

When they arrived at the gates of the camps themselves, they were told they would be given a mug of tea and then put to work. "But first, after your long journey, you must have a shower," they were told.

Exhausted, frightened, and terrorized though they were, parents with their children, sons and daughters with their mothers and fathers, simply could not imagine they were all about to be murdered.

The gas chambers were built to resemble showers. Signs in the anteroom instructed the Jews to remove their clothing and fold everything neatly so nothing would be lost. Then the people were taken into the "shower" rooms. The doors were shut and sealed. Cyanide gas poured out of the shower heads and the ventilators. Only then did the people realize that they were to be killed. Within four to five minutes the victims were dead.

Other Jewish prisoners were forced to remove the bodies, take them to the crematoria, and burn the remains. At Auschwitz, the ashes were often used to

Above: The Nazis forced Jews to sew yellow Stars of David like this on their clothing. The badge marked the Jews out from the rest of the population and made them even more vulnerable.

Opposite: The Jews' Last Road was painted by Waldemar Nowakowski, a Jewish victim of the Nazis at Auschwitz. It is a humiliating picture — but then the death of six million Jews in those circumstances was humiliating. The picture shows how men, women, and children were sent naked and demeaned to their death.

This picture, called The Roll Call, *was drawn by Wincenty Gawron in Auschwitz in 1942.*

"Every roll call was a selection: women were sent to the gas chamber because they had swollen legs, scratches on their bodies, because they wore eyeglasses or head kerchiefs. Young SS men prowled among the inmates and took down their numbers and during the evening roll call the women were ordered to step forward, and we never saw them again."

Lena Berg,
survivor of the Holocaust

help pave the camp roads and sometimes sold locally as fertilizer. Sometimes so many people were killed that the crematoria could not keep up their work of disposal. Bodies were stacked in piles like cordwood. Often they were buried in mass graves. The Nazis massacred and tortured everywhere they went. Millions of non-Jewish civilians from every country the Nazis invaded were butchered. The Nazis also sent gypsies, Poles, Russians, homosexuals, and others to concentration camps and gas chambers. They murdered French and British prisoners of war. Jehovah's Witnesses, leading churchmen, and German political prisoners were also killed.

But the Jews were the only people marked out for *total* physical annihilation. Police forces and government officials in every Nazi-occupied country were ordered to find and send to a death camp every single Jew. The punishment for any non-Jew who tried to hide or help a Jew was death.

If the war had continued much longer, it is possible that no Jews would have been left alive in Nazi-occupied areas of Europe.

Resistance

It is often, unfairly, said that the Jews went meekly to their deaths. In fact, they often tried to resist. There were heroic revolts at Sobibor, Treblinka, and other camps. In 1943 the starved and pitifully few remnants of the Warsaw Ghetto, from which a third of a million Jews had already been taken and murdered, rose up against the Nazis in a suicidally brave uprising and even managed to hold out for four weeks before being overcome and killed.

The Jews resisted wherever and however they could. Sometimes even within the death camps, they flung themselves at their tormentors with their bare hands, only to be mowed down with machine guns and hand grenades. Many went to their deaths shouting defiance. "We today, you tomorrow!"

But the Jews were helpless, unarmed, and utterly alone in the middle of often hostile and usually indifferent local populations. They were also confronted by the most powerful and pitiless state on earth.

The world watches

The world was silent as thousands of Jews were murdered every day.

As the Jewish catastrophe unfolded between 1941 and 1945, most of the world just stood by and watched. The Nazis had tried, usually with great success, to keep their crimes secret. But the killings were on such a colossal scale and involved so many millions of people and hundreds of thousands of witnesses and accomplices that the secret could not be kept for long. From 1942 on, reports about what was happening to the Jews trickled out of Nazi-controlled Europe to reach the Allies and the outside world. Their reaction was, on the whole, shameful. Jewish pleas for help were almost totally ignored.

On one occasion, a callous British official described news of the killings and the desperate pleas from the Jews as "Jewish Agency sob stuff." In Palestine, the British stuck to their policy of keeping out desperate, fleeing Jews.

In 1942, the British even turned away a refugee ship

called the *Struma*, which sank soon afterward, killing all 769 Jews on board. The United States, with huge numbers of immigration quotas unfilled, kept its doors shut to hundreds of thousands of Jewish applicants desperate to find a refuge.

The brave few

And yet at this time of world indifference and Nazi persecution, there were also examples of astonishing goodness despite threats of punishment.

All over occupied Europe, thousands of brave, ordinary Christians quietly defied the Nazi terror by helping Jews. They risked their lives and the lives of their families by hiding Jews in their own homes or helping them to escape.

In Denmark, the whole nation from the king down refused to accept the Nazis' anti-Jewish laws, and all but a tiny fraction of the country's Jews were saved.

In Bulgaria, the church, the people, and the government resisted Nazi demands for action against the Jews. The Bulgarians simply refused to send the Jews to the Auschwitz death camp, and not a single death train left the country.

Even in fascist Italy, which was Germany's ally, many officials did their best to save Jewish lives.

These acts of heroism were few and far between.

And few deeds would be more extraordinary than the persistent efforts of Raoul Wallenberg to save Hungary's Jews.

By 1944, Raoul had seen firsthand much Jewish suffering in Nazi-occupied Europe. His job as director of the food import-export business run by Hungarian-Jewish refugee Koloman Lauer had taken him throughout Europe. Raoul was deeply distressed by what he had seen.

Most of his life was still spent in neutral, peaceful Sweden, where he was free to go to dances, have picnics, and simply enjoy himself. Although most people would have been happy to have been away from danger, Raoul was strangely restless. He spent a lot of time thinking and worrying about the Jews, but so far, he was powerless to do anything to help.

His friends noticed that he was restless. "He seemed

a little depressed," one friend remembered afterward. "I had the feeling he wanted to do something more worthwhile with his life." Later Raoul saw and was deeply impressed by an updated film version of *The Scarlet Pimpernel*, in which the hero almost effortlessly rescues people from the Nazis. "On the way home he told me that was just the kind of thing he would like to do," his half-sister said later.

Soon he would get his chance to do exactly that.

Hungary: the last Jews of Europe

By the beginning of 1944, most of the Jews of Europe were already dead.

Nearly three million Polish Jews alone had been slaughtered, and most of the smaller Jewish populations of the rest of Europe had also been devastated. The few Jews who survived had fled, were in hiding, or were being slowly worked and starved to death in ghettos and compulsory work camps.

Only one large Jewish community remained intact — the Jews of Germany's ally, Hungary. Now Hitler and his Nazi killers turned their attention to that country's 750 thousand Jews.

In March 1944, the chief Nazi executioner, Adolf Eichmann, was ordered to prepare the deportation and annihilation of Hungarian Jewry.

The gas chambers and crematoria at the largest of all the death factories, Auschwitz-Birkenau, were prepared. A new railroad sidetrack was built to take the victims to within a few yards of the slaughtering places. All was ready for the Hungarian Jews.

Adolf Eichmann

Eichmann, who was to become Raoul Wallenberg's archenemy in Hungary, is one of the most chilling figures in world history.

We often think of mass murderers as being grotesque, storybook monsters. But in Eichmann's case, the reality was much more frightening. He appeared on the surface to be normal. He was married and he was an ambitious government official who desperately wanted to be liked by his bosses.

A Jewish boy from Czechoslovakia. One-and-a-half million Jewish children were murdered by the Nazis during the Holocaust.

But his job was far from normal, and his ultimate boss was Hitler. Eichmann's task was to round up the Jews and send them to their death.

By the time the massacre of Hungarian Jews started, Eichmann was thirty-eight. He was already responsible for the deaths of hundreds of thousands of innocent people.

Eichmann was a thoroughly insignificant person, but he found a way of making himself important by joining the Nazi Party in 1932. Soon he was a member of the sinister, black-shirted SS, and he became a self-styled expert in "Jewish matters."

He was very good at his job, and by 1942 he had become a trusted right-hand man to Reinhard Heydrich, the Nazi official who devised the "Final Solution," as the Nazis called their plan to murder all the Jews.

Eichmann was proud to be put in charge of organizing the roundup and deportation of Jewish victims to Treblinka, Auschwitz, and the other death camps.

What made Eichmann unique was the eagerness he brought to his task. He pursued Jews with untiring zeal. Yet at his trial in Jerusalem in 1961, he claimed not to have disliked Jews. As far as he was concerned, he was just doing a job and obeying orders.

Many other callous Nazi officials felt the same way. Like the commandant of Auschwitz, for example, they would spend a day carrying out the execution of hundreds of innocent victims. And then they would go home to their families and play with their children as if nothing unusual had happened.

Eichmann seemed to have no sense of right or wrong at all. He greatly enjoyed his power of life and death over others. And having this power depended upon pleasing his Nazi masters. These masters, in turn, were desperate to win the praise of Adolf Hitler, the head of the whole depraved system.

Hitler said of the Jews, "They are our old enemy." He was determined to "uproot them from Europe." Only then, he believed, could the war end.

As soon as Eichmann arrived in Hungary, he set about his new task with relish. "You know who I am," he taunted Jewish leaders he had called together. "I am the one known as the bloodhound!"

Nazi bureaucrat Adolf Eichmann, architect of the Nazi "Final Solution" and Raoul Wallenberg's enemy in Budapest. He boasted of his speed and efficiency in sending millions of Jewish people to their deaths. The judge who finally sentenced him to death told him: "No member of the human race can be expected to want to share the earth with you."

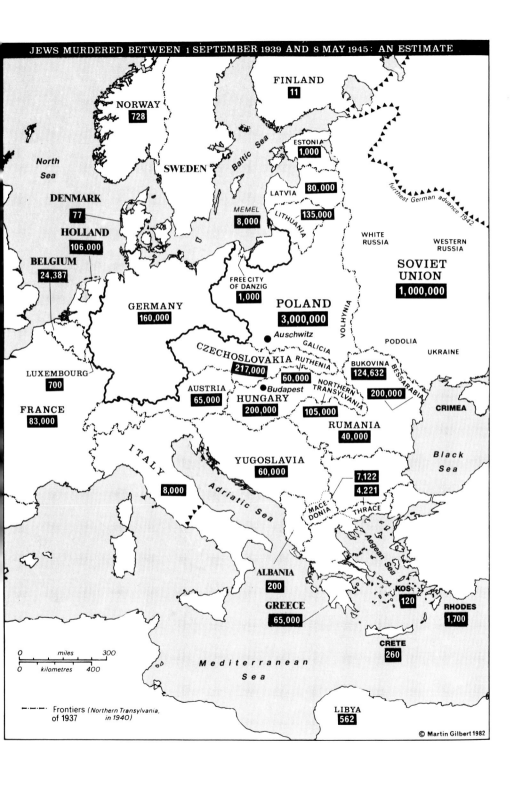

JEWS MURDERED BETWEEN 1 SEPTEMBER 1939 AND 8 MAY 1945: AN ESTIMATE

FINLAND
11

NORWAY
728

ESTONIA
1,000

North
Sea

SWEDEN

Baltic Sea

LATVIA
80,000

Furthest German advance 1942

DENMARK
77

MEMEL
8,000

LITHUANIA
135,000

WHITE
RUSSIA

WESTERN
RUSSIA

HOLLAND
106.000

BELGIUM
24,387

FREE CITY
OF DANZIG
1,000

SOVIET
UNION
1,000,000

GERMANY
160,000

POLAND
3,000,000

VOLHYNIA

PODOLIA

UKRAINE

Auschwitz

GALICIA

LUXEMBOURG
700

CZECHOSLOVAKIA
217,000

RUTHENIA

60,000

BUKOVINA
124,632

BESSARABIA

AUSTRIA
65,000

Budapest
HUNGARY
200,000

NORTHERN
TRANSYLVANIA
105,000

200,000

FRANCE
83,000

CRIMEA

RUMANIA
40,000

ITALY

YUGOSLAVIA
60,000

Black
Sea

8,000

Adriatic Sea

7,122

4,221

MACE-
DONIA

THRACE

Aegean Sea

ALBANIA
200

KOS
120

GREECE
65,000

RHODES
1,700

CRETE
260

0   miles   300

0   kilometres   400

Mediterranean
Sea

LIBYA
562

— · — · — Frontiers (Northern Transylvania,
of 1937   in 1940)

© Martin Gilbert 1982

All over Europe, Jews were dragged from their homes and put on death trains headed for the extermination camps. This painting by Chris Baeckman shows the arrest of a frightened Jewish family in Holland.

The Nazis move on Hungary

In Hungary, the extermination process was to be conducted at lightning speed. Years of practice had made Eichmann's killers experts in their deadly work. The machinery of deception and slaughter had reached new levels of sophistication.

The Nazis moved into Hungary in March 1944 and immediately began to take measures against the Jews. Jews were forced to hand over all their gold and valuables. In the Hungarian provinces, Jews were collected together in ghettos — the first stage of the journey to death.

At loading stations, Jews were jammed into cattle cars and the doors nailed shut for an agonizing journey. Each train carried thousands of people. The journey sometimes took five days without food or water. There were no sanitary arrangements at all. Many died or went insane. Periodically, the trains stopped so that dead bodies could be taken out.

From May 14, 1944, until July 8, the day before

"For many months now I have witnessed the suffering of the Hungarian people and, if it is not too presumptuous to say so, I think I have participated in it spiritually to such an extent that it has now become my suffering."
Raoul Wallenberg

Wallenberg arrived in Budapest, a total of 148 deportation trains left for the gas chambers at Auschwitz-Birkenau. On arrival, the Jews would be unloaded. Surrounded by guards, dogs, electrified barbed-wire fences, and machine-gun towers, a pitiless selection took place. Nazi guards and doctors chose a few fit-looking men and women for work or for cruel and pointless "medical experiments."

The rest of the Jews had no idea what was about to happen to them. All of them, including young children and old people, were sent straight to the gas chambers — and their deaths.

Then all the bodies were dragged away by Jewish slaves to be burned in the colossal, specially built crematoria housed in the same camp.

In the gas chambers and crematoria, six thousand men, women, and children each day would be murdered and burned. The operation took just a couple of hours. It was a highly efficient factory for killing large numbers of people.

Jews in hiding in a "safe house" in Budapest in 1944. Setting up the safe houses was one of Raoul Wallenberg's first actions when he arrived in Hungary that summer.

The deportations from Hungary continued at a brisk pace. The crematoria in Auschwitz-Birkenau operated at full speed. In a little less than two months, almost 450 thousand Hungarian Jewish men, women, and children were deported by the Nazis. Most of them were murdered.

Éva's diary

The terror of the time was poignantly captured by a thirteen-year-old girl, Éva Heyman, who kept a diary during the process of being rounded up and made ready for the death trains.

March 31: Éva tells how the Jews were being made to wear a yellow star patch. This was so that everyone would know they were different and despised. On April 7 she wrote about how she made a fuss when the police came to take her bicycle away. On April 20 most of the family's possessions were taken: telephone, radio, sewing machine, vacuum cleaner, camera, electric fryer.

Then, on May 5, Éva wrote: "Dear Diary, now you aren't at home anymore, but in the ghetto. Three days we waited for them to come and get us.... Dear Diary,

I'm still too little a girl to write down what I felt while we waited to be taken into the ghetto. Between one order and the next, Agi would cry out that we deserve what we get because we are like animals, patiently waiting to be slaughtered. . . . The two policemen who came weren't unfriendly; they just took Agi's and Grandma's wedding rings away from them. Agi was shaking all over and couldn't get the wedding ring off her finger."

By May 10, Éva Heyman is in the camp inside the ghetto. "Actually, everything is forbidden, but the most awful thing is that the punishment for everything is death." She later tells how her grandfather, a pharmacist, was giving poison from the ghetto pharmacy to the old people who wanted to die.

May 22: "Today they announced that every head of family will be taken in [to the Dreher brewery] so Grandpa also has to go. Terrific screaming comes from the direction of Dreher. All day long an electric gramophone keeps playing the same song — 'There's Just One Girl in the World.' Day and night the noise of this song fills the ghetto. When the record stops for a moment we can hear the yelling."

In her last diary entry, on May 30, Éva wrote: "Dear Diary, I don't want to die; I want to live." On June 2, 1944, she was crammed onto the train for Auschwitz, where she survived until October 17, when she was murdered in the gas chambers.

The United States reacts at last

By early 1944, the world's leaders knew precisely what was going on at Auschwitz and were fully aware that Hungary's Jews were about to be massacred. The stream of terrible news trickling out of Nazi-occupied Europe about the fate of the Jews became a flood.

The pressure for the Allies to do something — *anything* — to help the Jews became overwhelming.

In the United States, President Franklin D. Roosevelt had denounced the Nazi annihilation policy and promised that all who took part in it would be punished after the war. But the United States, which had locked its doors against the Jews before the war, did little to help them during it.

Perhaps one of Raoul Wallenberg's greatest achievements was to get a few members of the international community to work together to help the cornered Jews. The Red Cross, the Swiss embassy, the Dominican Republic, and some Christian groups would follow his example, producing hundreds of their own passports and organizing food supplies.

Many Jewish leaders in North America were bitter about what U.S. Secretary of the Treasury Henry Morgenthau, Jr., himself a Jew, called the "indifferent, callous and, perhaps, hostile" attitude of U.S. officials who had failed to take action to stop or slow down the slaughter. Meanwhile, many U.S. and British war strategists felt that the quickest way to save the most Jews was to win the war swiftly.

Under pressure, Roosevelt finally set up a new organization, the War Refugee Board, to do whatever was possible to help the Jews. The Board was to be an invaluable source of help and money for Raoul Wallenberg in his rescue work.

Raoul Wallenberg is chosen

The War Refugee Board needed someone to be sent into Hungary, where a brave person could possibly do

"Here is a man who had the choice of remaining in secure neutral Sweden when Nazism was ruling Europe. Instead, Wallenberg left this haven and went to what was then one of the most perilous places in Europe. And for what? To save Jews."
Gideon Hausner, Eichmann's prosecutor

something, anything, for the trapped Jews. U.S. officials approached Sweden for help, as it was the most important neutral country left in Europe and a country which still had reasonably good relations with the German government.

Sweden agreed. But who should be sent? Some officials thought an experienced diplomat should get the job. But the Jewish leaders were consulted, and when Koloman Lauer heard of the plan, he recommended Raoul Wallenberg.

Raoul eagerly accepted the mission to actively help the Jews of Hungary.

But he had a few extra conditions of his own. He knew that time was running out fast for the Jews. Nazi Budapest was a viper's nest. It was no place for ordinary diplomacy.

He would have to cut corners and bribe, cajole, and connive his way through official red tape if he needed to. There would be no time to check with the Swedish government. He demanded and was given diplomatic status and issued Swedish neutral passports to give to the Jews to make them appear Swedish and free them from persecution. He had enough money to provide safe houses and food for thousands, and even money to bribe officials.

By now it was the summer of 1944, and Wallenberg was desperately anxious to get to the Hungarian capital, Budapest. The news was so bad that many feared that soon there would be no Jews left for him to save.

Raoul reaches Hungary

On the day Raoul Wallenberg finally arrived in Budapest, the Nazis boasted that more than 400 thousand men, women, and children had been deported from the provinces. Only 230 thousand or so terrified Jews now remained alive in the capital.

The Germans knew they were losing the war. But the only question in Eichmann's mind was: could he empty the capital of Jews before the advancing Soviet armies took Budapest? For Wallenberg, the question was: how many Jews could he rescue before the capital was liberated?

Raoul Wallenberg's first job was to find a practical

Opposite, top: Eichmann's killers, aided by Hungarian gendarmes, continued to round up Jews and send them to the gas chambers at Auschwitz even while Wallenberg's daring rescue mission was being planned.

Opposite, bottom: Fascist ideas of authority and order had struck a chord in many countries, particularly those that, like Austria and Hungary, had been defeated in World War I. For these young Hungarian women seen here giving the Nazi salute, the German takeover of Hungary was not unwelcome.

"Wallenberg did not need to go. He went and proved that one man could make a difference."
Kati Marton,
from Wallenberg

way to help the Jewish people of Hungary — at once.

He hit upon a brilliant idea.

He knew that the ordinary German people had been educated to respect authority and to follow orders without question.

Now Wallenberg devised a plan to take advantage of this characteristic.

The *Schutz-pass*

He designed and printed a grand and impressive document that looked just like a passport. It carried the holder's photograph and was emblazoned with yellow and blue — like Sweden's national flag — and was full of official stamps and signatures. It looked tremendously official! But Wallenberg's new *Schutz-pass* (protection pass), as it was called, was actually a stupendous fake.

It had no legal status whatever. But that didn't matter. Because it looked so impressive, the Nazis believed it was genuine. They accepted its holders as Swedish citizens. Jews who held the Schutz-pass were now protected.

It was an inspired start, and soon Wallenberg's staff was turning out Schutz-passes as fast as possible. When he first arrived in Budapest, the Hungarian Foreign Ministry gave Wallenberg permission to issue fifteen hundred of these fake but priceless passports. Wallenberg gradually got the permitted quantity increased to five thousand by using clever threats and persuasion, and he actually issued over three times that many. To do this, he had to bribe and blackmail Hungarian officials to overlook the document's irregularity. In the final days, when he couldn't get any more printed, he issued a simplified document. Even this, although it was run off on poor-quality paper, sometimes worked wonders.

Other embassies in Budapest took their cue from Wallenberg's clever idea and began to follow suit with their own passes.

Getting the passes to threatened Jews became a priority. Wallenberg dashed out personally to distribute them at Budapest's railroad station. Within weeks thousands were saved with these fake documents. But they couldn't be given to everybody.

SCHUTZ-PASS

Nr. 65/44

Name: Név:	Frau Dr. Alfred Berndorfer geb. Vera Rosenfeld
Wohnort: Lakás:	Budapest
Geburtsdatum: Születési ideje:	7.VII.1920.
Geburtsort: Születési helye:	Miskolc
Körpergrösse: Magasság:	165 cm.
Haarfarbe: Hajszín: braun	Augenfarbe: Szeme: blau

Unterschrift:
Aláírás: *Vera Berndorfer*

SCHWEDEN ⚜ **SVÉDORSZÁG**

Die Kgl. Schwedische Gesandtschaft in Budapest bestätigt, dass der Obengenannte im Rahmen der — von dem Kgl. Schwedischen Aussenministerium autorisierten — Repatriierung nach Schweden reisen wird. Der Betreffende ist auch in einen Kollektivpass eingetragen.

Bis Abreise steht der Obengenannte und seine Wohnung unter dem Schutz der Kgl. Schwedischen Gesandtschaft in Budapest.

Gültigkeit: erlischt 14 Tage nach Einreise nach Schweden.

A budapesti Svéd Kir. Követség igazolja, hogy fennevezett — a Svéd Kir. Külügyminisztérium által jóváhagyott — repatriálás keretében Svédországba utazik. Nevezett a kollektív útlevélben is szerepel.

Elutazásig fennevezett és lakása a budapesti Svéd Kir. Követség oltalma alatt áll.

Érvényes vezeti a Svédországba való megérkezéstől számított tizennegyedik napon.

Reiseberechtigung nur gemeinsam mit dem Kollektivpass. Einreisenum wird nur in dem Kollektivpass eingetragen.

Budapest, den 22. Sept. 1944

KÖNIGLICH SCHWEDISCHE GESANDTSCHAFT
SVÉD KIRÁLYI KÖVETSÉG

Kgl.Schwedischer Gesandte

Above, left: Raoul Wallenberg's first stroke of genius was to design a grand-looking passport, the Schutz-pass, which would persuade the Nazis that the Hungarian Jews who carried them were protected by Sweden.

Above, right: The Schutz-pass was actually a stupendous fake — but this document saved thousands of lives.

Left: This piece of poor-quality paper issued by the Swedish embassy and signed by Raoul Wallenberg's colleague Per Anger saved Luise Havas's life. Her photograph is at the top of the document.

Hope

The Schutz-pass was visible proof that the Jews were not entirely friendless, and it was a means of saving thousands of Jewish lives. It was also a great morale-booster. One young woman to benefit was Edith Ernster, who later recalled that the passes "made us somehow feel like human beings again after being reduced to mere things by all the measures and propaganda against us."

Wallenberg knew how important morale was. In his first report to Stockholm he wrote, "The Jews are in despair. One way or another we must give them hope." Another time he wrote that it was "necessary to arouse the Jews from their apathy. We must get rid of their feeling that they have been abandoned."

Race against time

From the moment he arrived in Budapest on July 9, 1944, Wallenberg started a whirlwind of activity. He set up his humanitarian relief section, Section C, at the Swedish legation. Within weeks his staff expanded to four hundred people, mostly, if not all, Jews. Section C worked around the clock.

Huge deliveries of food were sent each day to the ghetto. During the following months Wallenberg's operation fed thousands of people each day.

All Jews were ordered to wear a conspicuous yellow Star of David. Yet Raoul, revealing his formidable qualities as a negotiator, managed to persuade the authorities to let the Jews working for him go without wearing the star.

Raoul Wallenberg did not cut a particularly charismatic or imposing figure. He was small and slight and was almost bald, but everyone who met him at that time was touched by his warmth and his great intelligence. He worked like a man inspired, sleeping only about four hours a night, generating incredible energy and optimism all around him.

He quickly established a formidable reputation, and even the local Nazis began to respect him. Wallenberg made an electrifying impression.

On one incredible occasion, a deportation train was about to leave for Auschwitz from the railroad station.

Suddenly Wallenberg climbed up on the roof of the train and started to hand hundreds of Schutz-passes to the Jews inside. He ignored the orders of the SS and did not stop, even when the guards shot over his head. Calmly, he walked from one car to the other until the last passport had been issued. Then Wallenberg ordered all pass-holders to leave the train and go to a caravan of autos bearing Sweden's colors. The Nazis seemed too stunned to do anything. The Jews were taken to safety.

Meanwhile, international pressure on the Hungarian leader, Admiral Miklós Horthy, who had earlier in the war resisted Nazi demands for tougher measures against the Jews, was mounting. The United States, Sweden, and Britain, in addition to the Pope and the International Red Cross, insisted on an end to the deportations. Horthy suspended the death trains.

Horthy had also withdrawn sixteen hundred brutal and much-feared Hungarian gendarmes whom Eichmann was using to round up Jews and put them on death trains.

Jews were sent to the death camps by train, locked inside small, filthy cattle cars. As many as a hundred victims were packed into each wagon without food or water. Many died or went insane on the journey to the death camp.

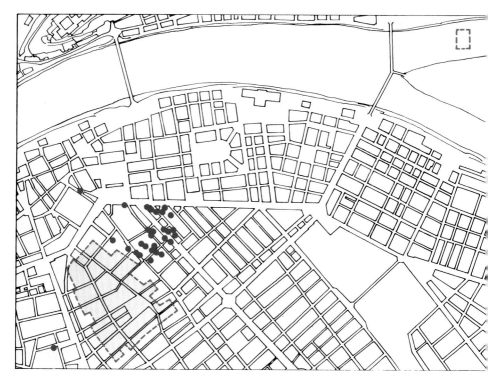

Above: This map of Budapest shows the position of the Jewish ghetto in 1945. Raoul Wallenberg had also arranged for thirty "safe houses" (indicated by purple dots) to be set up. The Swedish flag on each house gave some protection to the Jews taking refuge inside. Raoul had to organize food and medical help for the thirty-five thousand people who were crowded into them.

Relief work

With the deportations suspended for the moment at least, Wallenberg concentrated on relief work to reduce suffering. He began to set up hospitals, orphanages, and soup kitchens and bought huge quantities of food, medicine, and clothing, which he hid in different parts of the city. These would prove vital.

But Jews were still being dragged from their homes or picked off the streets by armed gangs of Hungarian Nazis. To counter this, Wallenberg had another brilliant idea. He set up "safe houses" where pass-holders could live protected by the Swedish government. Soon the Swedish flag hung outside these houses alongside the Jewish Star of David. Swiss and International Red Cross officials followed Wallenberg's example and did the same thing. As a result, thousands more lives were saved, even though the buildings were not always respected.

One admiring diplomat remarked about Raoul, after the war, "He accomplished feats that no other twenty

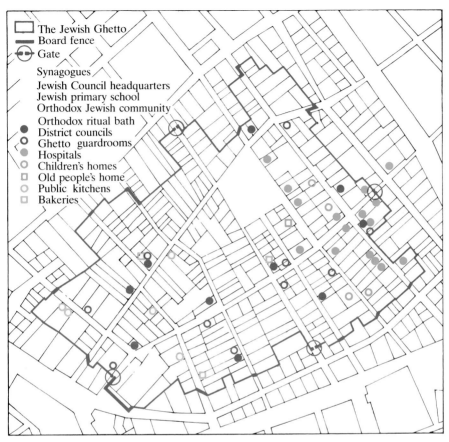

The Jewish Ghetto
Board fence
Gate

Synagogues
Jewish Council headquarters
Jewish primary school
Orthodox Jewish community
Orthodox ritual bath
District councils
Ghetto guardrooms
Hospitals
Children's homes
Old people's home
Public kitchens
Bakeries

Above: A detailed plan of the Jewish ghetto in 1945. Sixty thousand Jews had been taken from their homes and penned into this run-down area.

Left: A modern picture of the Swedish embassy in Budapest. In 1945 Raoul Wallenberg turned it into a "safe house" to protect Jews. To hundreds of Jews this was a refuge from the terror of the streets outside.

War-ravaged Budapest fell into lawless chaos during the last months of Nazi rule. Armed mobs of Nazi and Arrow Cross killers roamed the streets looking for Jews to torture and kill. Hitler's grand design would finally end in crushing defeat of Germany and its allies. Like most of the beautiful cities of Europe, Budapest was devastated.

diplomats in the world would even have attempted."

Per Anger, a Swedish colleague on Wallenberg's staff in Budapest, recalled the impression Wallenberg made on those who worked with him: "To start with, he shocked some of us professional diplomats by his unconventional methods, but we very soon found he had the right approach."

Wallenberg's rescue tactics were undiplomatic, to say the least: bribery, blackmail, and threats. But he was saving thousands of people's lives. He put his life on the line time and time again.

Bridges at high levels

One of Wallenberg's tactics was to get to know important people who could help him in his urgent mission of rescuing the Jews.

Dr. Istvan Szondy, still working as a dentist on Ulloi Street in 1987, remembers Wallenberg well. "He was strong in his soul. I can see him sitting drinking his favorite wine — Bull's Blood. He was a short man, good-looking, with a thin neck and a large Adam's apple. He wore well-tailored suits. In October 1944 he opened an office here. He turned the second floor into a Swedish safe house for the Jews. There were 270 Jews living here.

"He tried to build bridges at a high level," Dr. Szondy said years later. "I had a patient at the time called Zoltan Bagossy who was the deputy foreign minister. He knew that the war was lost, and when I introduced him to Raoul he asked for Swedish protection for himself and his son against the Soviets. Wallenberg promised to help if Bagossy would in turn help protect 'his' Jews. They shook hands on the deal. A short while after, 250 of the Jews living here were seized. Fortunately someone put through a call from my surgery to Bagossy and they were returned to us very quickly."

By October 1944, the combination of Wallenberg's work inside Budapest and Allied pressure from outside had forced the Hungarian dictator Horthy to establish a more moderate government. This government had been able to get the Germans to agree that Eichmann and his death squads would leave Hungary.

Wallenberg thought his work was over. He began shutting down his rescue operation and thinking of going home to Sweden in time for Christmas.

The Arrow Cross terror

By now, Horthy was desperately anxious to get out of the war, but on October 15, 1944, the day he planned to announce Hungary's surrender to the Allies, the murderous Hungarian Nazi party, known as the Arrow Cross, seized power in a coup. This was a terrible blow for the Jews.

Now a fresh wave of violence more terrible than before hit Budapest. Many Jews committed suicide. Jewish yellow-star homes were sealed and nobody was allowed in or out for ten days. Many starved to death. Raoul would not be home for Christmas after all. In fact, he would never see his family again.

Hardly anybody showed up for work at his relief office. The terrified staff had gone into hiding. Wallenberg borrowed a woman's bicycle and rode around town to his workers' homes, trying to rally their spirits and to get them to come to work.

Later, Wallenberg discovered that his personal

"Wallenberg never tired and was at work day and night. He saved human lives, traveled, bargained, threatened the interruption of diplomatic relations, was in consultation with the Hungarian government — in short achieved something that makes him a sort of legendary figure."
Samu Stern, wartime Hungarian Jewish leader

driver, Vilmos Langfelder, had been taken to Arrow
Cross headquarters. Right away Wallenberg went to
the grim and intimidating building and demanded
Langfelder's release. Wallenberg spoke with such
authority that startled Arrow Cross men actually let
Langfelder go!

When Wallenberg heard that thousands of Jews
were being held in the synagogue on Dohány Street, he
contacted the Swiss consul, Charles Lutz, and together
they went to the synagogue to demand the release of
the Swedish and Swiss pass-holders. "They are
Swedish citizens," he shouted in German to the young
Hungarian Arrow Cross guards. "I order you to
release them."

Wallenberg ordered his "Swedes" to form a line.
Behind them a group of "Swiss" began to gather. Then
with great assurance Wallenberg marched his people
out of the synagogue, followed by Lutz at the head of
his "Swiss" Jews. In response to combined international protest, the rest of the hostages were freed
shortly after. It was a tremendous victory for sheer
nerve and courage, and it put some heart back into the
shocked and bewildered Jewish people.

The death marches

Eichmann had returned to Budapest after the Arrow
Cross takeover. He had immediately summoned local
Jewish leaders. "I am back," he taunted them. "Our
arm is still long enough to reach you."

No trains would leave Hungary for the death camps
now. Eichmann had devised a demonic alternative
method for transferring the Jews.

He would march Jewish men, women, and children
out of the city and to the border at gunpoint. Trains
waiting at the other side of the border would take the
Jews on to Auschwitz. These forced marches in the
freezing sleet and snow came to be known as the
"death marches."

Anyone who fell by the roadside was either shot or
beaten to death.

As soon as he heard of Eichmann's plans, Wallenberg vowed to fight for the rights of protective pass-
holders. His office began producing hundreds of

*A Jewish family arrives at
the death factory of
Auschwitz. Women and
children were almost
always murdered within a
few hours of arrival. Soon
after this picture was taken
by SS guards, these
children and their mother
were gassed and their
bodies burned in the death
camp's crematoria.*

letters of protest to government departments. He still used diplomatic language but there was often a threat behind his words. He warned Hungarian officials that if they helped with the persecution of the Jews they could be hanged after the war as war criminals. Wallenberg's staff was also continually busy trying to trace missing Jews.

Unimaginable suffering

The death marches began on November 8, 1944. Children, women, and old men were all forced to march through the slush for days without food or water. At night they just dropped to the ground in utter exhaustion. Some froze to death. Many committed suicide, some by throwing themselves into the icy waters of the Danube. Bodies lay along the route of the march and hung from trees. The suffering of these doomed people was unimaginable.

Miriam Herzog was seventeen at the time. She remembers: "The gendarmes were brutal, beating those who could not keep up, leaving others to die in the ditches. . . . There were some good people in Hungary, but the gendarmes were absolute animals. I hate them even worse than the Germans. At one point along the road we met a convoy of German soldiers going the other way, towards the front. Ordinary Wehrmacht men, not SS. When they saw how the Hungarian gendarmes were treating us, they appeared to be horrified. 'You'll be all right when you get to Germany. . . . We don't treat women like this there.' I can only suppose that they did not know about the extermination camps."

Time and again, with extraordinary courage, Wallenberg and his helpers drove out into the snow to give food, help, and encouragement to the exhausted, suffering Jews on the marches and to save them wherever and however he could.

In 1980, one survivor of the terrible ordeal, Zvi Eres, recorded his memories for television. He recalled "a foreigner" on the road near the frontier. That foreigner was Wallenberg.

"He ordered one of his colleagues to note our names. When we reached the frontier at Hegyeshalom

"We were so tired that we fell down and we slept on the earth. And in the night it was frost and in the morning we got up and many of the women were dead. We got something every third or fourth day, soup or something, and the worst of all was that they didn't give us a drink and do you know to march and not to drink was a most terrible thing."

Miriam Herzog, survivor of the Holocaust

A death march. Jews were now forced to march hundreds of miles to their deaths through snow and bitter cold.

"Wallenberg made me feel human again. For the first time I had hope. . . . He showed us that we were not animals, that someone cared about us. And the point of it was that he came himself, he came personally. He stopped for us, for each of us. . . ."

Susan Tabor,
survivor of the Holocaust

we were sent to a stable when we were told that this foreigner, Wallenberg, was trying to rescue us from the death march."

Wallenberg shouted at the German and Hungarian officers to have his pass-holders released while colleagues like Per Anger were secretly handing out more passports to people in the crowd. Anyone showing the confused guards any kind of document, even a scrap of paper, would be accepted as a Swedish pass-holder amid the chaos.

Per Anger remembers Wallenberg's methods when addressing the exhausted, starving, demoralized Jews, trying to get them to claim to be Swedish. "He was rather like an auctioneer trying to get people to bid: 'Look, are there any who have Swedish passports?' And then he sort of bluffed: 'Would you have one, and you there? — yes, certainly.' And so we got back a

couple of hundred that time, many who didn't have protective passes at all!"

Miriam Herzog was lying exhausted on the floor of the Swedish hut at the Hungarian border from where the trains left for Auschwitz. She remembers Wallenberg entering the stinking hut, which was full of dirty, exhausted, and starving people. He seemed to have come from a dream because he was very elegant, very well-dressed, and very handsome. "I asked 'Who is this gentleman?' because everyone hated us and all the world was against us and his coming in smiling and wanting to help, and he told us 'I want to save you all.'"

Despite all his efforts, his tireless energy, and his bravery, Wallenberg could save only a relatively small number of people on the death marches — thousands out of hundreds of thousands. The death marches continued until late November 1944, when international protests finally stopped them.

Thousands of children and women died of exhaustion or were shot or beaten to death on the death marches.

But the suffering and danger for the Jewish people was not yet over.

The death marches stopped. But the death trains began again.

Hell on earth

In the last days of the Nazi occupation, the staff at the Swedish embassy organized a party to celebrate Raoul's incredible mission to save the Jews. They prepared a magnificent folding Christmas card. It was a spoof of art through the ages — each picture showing Raoul Wallenberg and his Schutz-passes. The original of this mosaic showed Saint George fighting the dragon. Instead Raoul holds out a Schutz-pass.

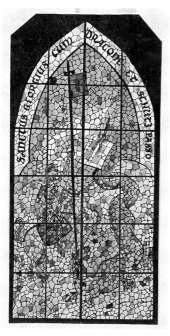

In November of that year Budapest slipped into a state of lawlessness.

Gangs of crazed, leaderless Arrow Cross killers roamed the streets, breaking into Swiss and Swedish "safe houses" and murdering Jews. Even babies were not spared. Hospitals were broken into and patients dragged out and shot. One gang was led by a mad priest, András Kun, who carried a gun in one hand and a crucifix in the other. Kun organized a mass execution at a Jewish hospital in Buda where many staff members and patients were murdered. A sadistic woman, Mrs. Vilmos Salzer, led her band of killers with a machine gun in her hands and took delight in torturing Jewish women to death.

Many Jews who were found were taken to the banks of the Danube River, tied together, and shot and dumped into the freezing water. As they floated away, the Arrow Cross killers sometimes used their bobbing heads for target practice.

Throughout the city, the streets were strewn with the bodies of slain Jews.

Israeli broadcaster Tommy Lapid later recorded his memories for a recent British television documentary about Raoul Wallenberg: "I sometimes think that the greatest achievement of the Nazis was that we accepted the fact that we, as a people, were supposed to be killed. We didn't think twice about the absurdity of the fact that somebody was trying to kill us just because of our religion. It was the victory of the Nazi terror that we considered ourselves potentially victims for murder."

Tommy Lapid described how his mother was rescued by Wallenberg. "He was a legend among the Jews," Lapid recalls. "In the framework of the complete hell in which we lived there was a savior angel somewhere moving around and saving lives. My mother told me that, as they were being taken down to the river, a car arrived and out stepped Wallenberg. He went after these Hungarians and protested and said these people were under his protection.

"They quarreled with him and he must have had some charisma, personal authority, because there was absolutely nothing behind him. He must have been the loneliest man in the world, trying to pretend there was something behind him. They could have shot him there in the street and nobody would have known about it, but they relented. . . ."

Lapid continued, "Two or three hours later, to my amazement, my mother returned with the other women. It seemed like a mirage, a miracle. My mother was there — and she was alive and she was hugging me and kissing me, and she said one word: 'Wallenberg.'"

"This is why I cherish his memory to this very day."

Wallenberg rushed out whenever he heard Jewish people were in danger. In 1987, the Chief Rabbi of Budapest, Dr. Odon Zinger, recalled how another of Wallenberg's daring, almost reckless, acts saved Dr. Zinger's brother, along with several hundred other Jewish men.

"I asked Wallenberg for a passport for my brother,

Another section of the card made for the same Christmas party shows Raoul receiving one of his own lifesaving Schutz-passes.

45

who was in a compulsory work camp. He not only gave me a passport for my brother but a hundred more for the other imprisoned workers. One day, one of the prisoners came with a policeman — a proper police-man, not the Arrow Cross — and told us the workers were being taken away. Wallenberg seized his book listing the pass-holders and we jumped into his car and tore off with flags flying. When we got to the camp, Wallenberg shouted out: 'Let free the Swedish citi-zens. How dare you deport Swedish pass-holders! Sweden is a neutral country which represents Ger-many in many countries of the world,' he cried.

"He called out the names of the pass-holders and they lined up behind him. As he collected the pass-ports he quietly put them into my hand and I secretly gave them out again to other deportees.

"That day we saved about six hundred people with only one hundred passports!"

In some ways, the Jews in the protected houses or those living in hiding with false documents were even more at risk. The Arrow Cross did not respect the Swiss, Swedish, and Red Cross homes, even though they were clearly marked with large Red Cross signs and notices.

There were nightly raids. Men were stripped to discover whether they were circumcised. Thousands were dragged off screaming, lined up, and shot.

Fear in the ghettos

There were now two ghettos in Budapest. More than sixty thousand Jews were packed into the larger one, the Central Ghetto, with the town's three main syna-gogues. The smaller International Ghetto was made up of all the different "safe houses" belonging to the Swedes, the Swiss, and the International Red Cross.

The city was filled with fear — fear of the black-booted, green-shirted Arrow Cross thugs who raided in the night and dragged people away to be murdered; fear of the gendarmes who might come to take Jews to the railroad station; and fear, too, of the German soldiers who executed people on the spot.

The Jews felt abandoned — the world seemed to have forgotten them.

Starvation, disease, and depression were rampant. And it was freezing cold.

Furniture had to be cut up for firewood. There were quarrels in the ghetto over food. People who became mentally ill often had to be restrained. There was terrible overcrowding, with hardly a place to sit or lie down. Many died in the ghetto in those dreadful last weeks of 1944.

The fate of the remaining Jews of Budapest now rested on the outcome of the battle of wills between two utterly different men — Adolf Eichmann and Raoul Wallenberg.

The fanatical Nazi Adolf Eichmann, backed up by thousands of soldiers and police, was still determined to kill every last Jew in the city.

Wallenberg, gentle and bearing the conscience of the world on his slim shoulders, was equally determined to stop the slaughter.

Eichmann wanted Wallenberg dead. But Wallenberg was protected. He was a senior Swedish diplomat, and Eichmann could not touch him without damaging Germany's relations with Sweden, a relationship which Nazi leaders were anxious to preserve.

Raoul Wallenberg briefing his helpers in his Budapest office in November 1944. Wallenberg recruited many of Budapest's finest community leaders and business experts onto his team. He gained for them the right to dispense with wearing a yellow star because they were employees of a neutral mission. That alone meant that many lives were saved.

Encounter with Eichmann

Eichmann had already threatened to kill Wallenberg. He had told someone at the Red Cross office, "I will kill that Jew-dog Wallenberg!"

That a meeting should take place between Wallenberg and Eichmann was extraordinary. Yet it did — Wallenberg invited his archenemy to dinner.

Wallenberg thought he might be able to persuade or frighten Eichmann into giving up his drive against the Jews. Wallenberg knew that the Soviets were only a few weeks, at most, away from Budapest. He also knew that all the Jewish people in the ghettos could be killed in the days or even the hours before the advancing Soviet armies arrived.

The dinner, with lavish food and wine, took place in a wealthy nobleman's house which Raoul borrowed for the occasion. At the end of the meal, Wallenberg rose and switched off the lights. He then had the curtains drawn open to show the approaching Soviet guns flashing and a sky reddened by fire, proof that the Nazi reign of terror was about to end. He then amazed his guest by launching into an attack on Nazism. Eichmann could not really answer Wallenberg's argument. All he could say was that he still enjoyed his power and hoped to have it for a little while longer. Eichmann lived in luxury. His power as mass executioner enabled him to extort almost anything he wanted from his victims, including fine china, glassware, and works of art.

Lars Berg, an embassy colleague of Wallenberg's who witnessed this extraordinary encounter, recalled, "Eichmann declared that when the Soviets came they would shoot him: 'I am the head of the SS in Hungary; I will be given no pardon.' Then he said very quietly, very politely, to Wallenberg, 'Well, even if I think you're right, don't think we're friends. You have a Swedish diplomatic passport but I'm not sure it will protect you. Even a neutral diplomat can meet with an accident.' After that Eichmann rose, very quietly thanked Wallenberg for the dinner, bowed and left."

A few days later, a large German truck drove straight into Wallenberg's car and completely destroyed it. Fortunately, he was not inside.

Wallenberg invited Eichmann to dinner at a nobleman's house — and then launched an attack on Nazi ideology. Eichmann was dumbfounded. He threatened to have Wallenberg murdered. This illustration of the famous encounter, by W. C. Burgard, was commissioned for a special magazine edition produced in memory of Wallenberg.

Dead or alive

By late December 1944, the Soviets had almost reached the city. In these last days of the siege of Budapest, Wallenberg was on the run himself. There was a price on his head. Death threats now came his way. Every night he hid in a different place. He changed his license plates constantly. Yet he saved even more lives than ever.

Wallenberg seemed inspired. Resourceful as ever, he had made valuable police contact — a member of the Arrow Cross, Pál Szálai, who was revolted by the slaughter and kept Wallenberg informed of planned murder squad raids. He even gave Wallenberg a police bodyguard.

Per Anger remembers his last meeting with Wallenberg during these desperate final days: "While bombs were exploding all around us, we set out on a visit to SS headquarters, where, among other things, I was to request some kind of shelter for embassy members. We had to stop the car repeatedly because the road was blocked with dead people, horses, burned-out trucks, and debris from bombed houses. But danger did not stop Wallenberg. I asked him whether he was afraid. 'It is frightening at times,' he said, 'but I have no choice. I have taken upon myself this mission and I would never be able to return to Stockholm without knowing that I have done everything that stands in a man's power to rescue as many Jews as possible.'"

The Central Ghetto miracle

By the end of December, the Soviets had surrounded Budapest. The Arrow Cross leader had fled the city. Eichmann himself left the city the day before Christmas Eve. But before he went he was determined to commit a final act of mass murder. He ordered the massacre of the more than ninety thousand Jews in the Central and International ghettos.

Incredibly, Wallenberg would foil him.

Raoul Wallenberg was about to perform his final miraculous act of rescue.

Szálai, Wallenberg's police contact, sent news of the planned massacre. Five hundred German soldiers and twenty-two Arrow Cross men were getting ready

"Wallenberg was the only foreign diplomat to stay behind in Pest, with the sole purpose of protecting these people. And he succeeded beyond all expectations. If you add them all up, 100,000 or more people owed their lives to him."

Per Anger, Wallenberg's colleague in Budapest

49

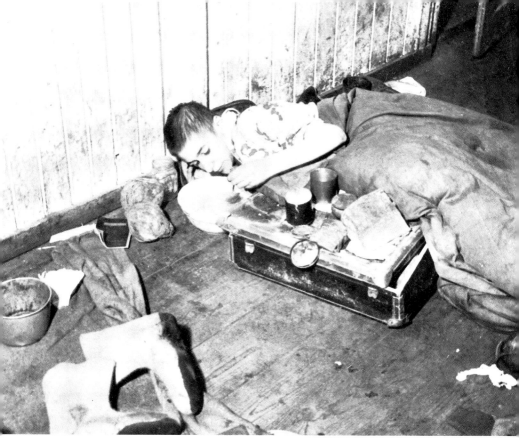

to kill everyone in the Central Ghetto. Two hundred Hungarian gendarmes were about to join them.

By now, it was too dangerous for Wallenberg to go himself. But he immediately sent a message to SS General August Schmidthuber, the man Eichmann had ordered to carry out the massacre, warning him: "If you do not stop this now, I can guarantee you will be hanged as a war criminal." Schmidthuber delayed a decision for several minutes, then backed down. The Jews of Budapest were spared.

The Soviets arrive

In January 1945, the nightmare of Nazi Budapest finally came to an end. The Soviet army entered the tortured city and halted the Nazi terror. The "Final Solution" was ended at last.

Yet in this hour of triumph, the incredible story of

Raoul Wallenberg was about to take a tragic twist.

By any reckoning, his achievements over the previous six months had qualified him as one of the bravest and greatest heroes of the entire war. He had daringly performed not one but hundreds of miracles and rescued no fewer than 100 thousand Jews — many of them several times over.

He should have been treated as a great hero. Yet, to the new rulers of Budapest, the Soviets, he seemed to be a criminal.

The drive to Debrecen

Raoul Wallenberg was blissfully unaware of this new danger to himself. In November, as the inevitable Nazi defeat drew nearer, he had started to think about how to help the Jews *after* the war.

He had set up a small department to begin planning how to find missing people and reunite scattered families. Food and medicine would be needed for the orphanages, ghettos, and safe houses where many people were nearly starving. Housing, bedding, furniture — Raoul had plans for everything needed to restore normal life.

When the Soviets arrived, he wanted to discuss these ambitious plans with them. Wallenberg and his driver, Vilmos Langfelder, obtained Soviet permission to see Marshal Rodion Malinovsky at his headquarters at Debrecen, 120 miles (193 km) east of Budapest. Wallenberg's assistants begged him not to go because they thought the meeting was too dangerous. But Wallenberg was in high spirits.

"I am going to meet the Russians. I have money with me and will try to help the Jews," he said.

When the Soviets came, Wallenberg left with them, carrying a large briefcase which probably contained a considerable sum of money with which he hoped to buy supplies and bribe officials. He may also have been carrying important documents.

Wallenberg smiled, waved, climbed into the waiting car, and was driven away. No one knew it at the time, but it was his final farewell.

The day was January 17, 1945. His friends and colleagues would never see him again.

Opposite, top: By 1945, Hitler had lost the war and British, American, and Soviet armies at last swept across Europe and liberated the few survivors of the Nazi extermination and concentration camps. This Jewish child is eating her first hot meal in a camp in freedom.

Opposite, bottom: Yet the Nazis continued to murder Jews right up until the very last moments. This pile of bones and ashes of victims from the ovens of one of the smaller camps, Buchenwald, measured six feet (2 m) in height.

Raoul disappears

What happened to Raoul Wallenberg next remains a tragic mystery.

Some facts are clear. Instead of listening to his plans, the Soviets promptly arrested him.

We do not know whether Wallenberg even reached Marshal Malinovsky's headquarters. He was probably picked up by the NKVD, the Soviet secret police, on the way. They might have thought he was a spy.

Released Soviet prisoners began to report that Wallenberg and his driver were locked up in the notorious Lubianka prison in Moscow no later than January or February 1945. But as the weeks and months, and then years, went by, many people, particularly his friends, the Jews in Budapest, began to think he was dead.

Forgotten hero

The governments of the free world had cared little about the suffering of the Jews during the war until it was too late to save most of them. In the years that followed, they were to prove that they cared even less about the Jews' greatest savior, Raoul Wallenberg.

If they had made loud and strong diplomatic protests about Wallenberg's fate in 1945 — in other words, as soon as people realized he was in trouble — it might well have been enough to save him.

But, shamefully, both the Swedish government, whose citizen and representative he was, and the United States, on whose behalf he had acted, failed to make a big effort to find Raoul Wallenberg.

The years dragged by and, almost incredibly, the hero of Budapest became a forgotten man, languishing in Soviet prisons. On August 18, 1947, the Soviet Union's senior deputy foreign minister, Andrei Vishinsky, sent a note to the Swedish government, claiming that Wallenberg was not to be found. "Wallenberg is not in the Soviet Union and . . . is unknown to us," he wrote.

Soviet lies

But the Soviets had already given several quite different versions of the story.

In February 1945, the Soviet ambassador to Sweden, Alexandra Kollontai, had announced that Wallenberg was in the Soviet Union. A month later, Soviet-controlled Kossuth Radio claimed that Raoul Wallenberg had been murdered by Hungarian fascists or "agents of the Gestapo."

Somewhere along the line, the Soviets were obviously lying.

In 1956, Soviet officials claimed that a thorough investigation confirmed that Wallenberg was not and never had been in the Soviet Union.

A year later, Soviet deputy foreign minister Andrei Gromyko gave a different version of the story, which the Soviet government has stuck to ever since — Wallenberg died of a heart attack in a Soviet prison in 1947 and his body was cremated.

But in the years that followed, it became clear that Wallenberg was still very much alive. Former Soviet prisoners said that they had spoken to Wallenberg, and that he was rotting away alone in a prison cell somewhere in the Soviet Union.

Between 1947 and 1980 there were reports that he had been seen at no fewer than fifteen different prisons, camps, and psychiatric hospitals in which political prisoners are often held and sometimes tortured.

Did the Soviets think Raoul was a spy?

There are several theories about why the Soviets locked up Wallenberg.

The Soviet Union had played a vital role in defeating Hitler, and its people had suffered horribly. But its government, under the dictator Joseph Stalin, was brutal and suspicious.

What were the Soviets to make of this young man, Raoul Wallenberg, who came from an aristocratic Swedish family and who carried with him vast amounts of money and, quite possibly, important documents and jewels? Were they really to believe he was on a humanitarian mission to save the Jews? From what they had seen in Hungary, Poland, and the Soviet Union itself, they probably believed that few people, if any, cared about the Jews.

The Soviets had other reasons for suspicion. Raoul's

This monument to Wallenberg's heroic struggle, commissioned by the Jews of Budapest, was dragged away by Soviet troops on the night before it was due to be unveiled in April 1948. It now stands outside a drug factory at Debrecen. Visitors are told it symbolizes humanity's struggle against disease. The snake originally had a Nazi swastika on its head. (Sculptor: Pál Palzai)

banking family had kept up contact with Germany during the war. Also, Wallenberg's main contact in the United States, War Refugee Board representative Iver Olsen, was a United States secret agent. This was unknown to Wallenberg, but probably known to the Soviets.

Years later, one of Wallenberg's colleagues, Lars Berg, offered this theory: "As soon as he got into contact with the Soviets he told them he wasn't only a Swedish diplomat but he was sent by President Roosevelt himself: he was working with American money to save Jewish lives. I think that's why he disappeared. It wasn't good at that time to declare you worked for the Americans."

During the war, the Soviet Union and the United States were allies against Hitler. But as the end of the war drew near, in 1945, the battle lines for their postwar conflict were being drawn.

Unwittingly, Raoul Wallenberg had stepped into a political minefield.

After many years had gone by, widespread international concern did finally begin to grow — thanks largely to the ceaseless efforts of Wallenberg's mother, Maj von Dardel, to find out what had happened to her missing son.

In the late 1970s and early 1980s, there were several books and films about the forgotten hero.

The Budapest Jews remember

The Jews of Budapest did not forget their savior.

After the war, despite their difficulties and hardships of all kinds, the Jews of Budapest set up a committee to collect funds for a Wallenberg memorial. The Hungarian sculptor Pál Palzai was commissioned to undertake the work. Palzai wanted to show a heroic figure struggling with a serpent — a serpent with a swastika on its head.

By April 1948, Palzai's great statue was ready. But the night before the unveiling ceremony, Soviet soldiers arrived with horses and dragged the statue away.

The memorial was later found in a Budapest basement. Without consulting those who had paid for it, authorities removed all references to Wallenberg

Above: Raoul's mother, Maj von Dardel.

Opposite: Artist's idea of Raoul in a Soviet prison.

Below: Wallenberg memorial, Budapest, 1987.

Wallenberg made sure that Jewish life survived in Hungary. The Jews in Budapest are now the only large Jewish community left in eastern Europe.

and also the swastika from the serpent's head. The monument was then set up outside a drug factory in Debrecen. Visitors are told that the statue represents humanity's struggle with disease, not that it celebrates Wallenberg's triumph over Nazism.

Until 1987 there was only one small official reminder of Wallenberg in Hungary: a short, nondescript street renamed "Wallenberg Street" which runs close to the Danube. It was on this street in the heart of the International Ghetto that Wallenberg's Section C had rented houses as refuges for people it was protecting.

In 1987, the Hungarian government finally allowed the Wallenberg Monument by Imre Varga to be unveiled in Budapest.

The people of Israel remember

After the war, many Hungarian and other Jews settled in Israel. They were eager to see Wallenberg's heroism remembered, so they named a street in Jerusalem after him. He is also remembered at Yad Vashem, the Israeli Holocaust memorial, where, in 1979, a tree was planted in his memory in the Avenue of the Righteous. This avenue of trees celebrates non-Jews who risked their lives to save Jews. The ceremony was delayed until after the death of Wallenberg's mother. In the absence of proof, she had always refused to acknowledge that her son was dead.

There is another memorial and a recreation area, dedicated to Wallenberg, in the Jerusalem forest outside Yad Vashem. Wallenberg was also made Israel's first honorary citizen.

Above: Dr. Odon Zinger, Chief Rabbi of Budapest.

Below: Demonstrators demanding that the Soviets release Wallenberg.

The world remembers

All over the world, countries have acted to commemorate Wallenberg and his work. The states of New York and New Jersey declared a Raoul Wallenberg Day. The most remarkable of all the tributes to Wallenberg was honorary U.S. citizenship awarded by the United States Congress in 1981. True, Wallenberg had acted as the servant of U.S. agencies, the War Refugee Board, and U.S. Jewish relief organizations. Still, honorary citizenship was quite exceptional. Only once before had such an award ever been made: to the United States' staunch wartime ally, Winston Churchill.

But perhaps what Wallenberg himself would have regarded as his greatest memorial is the survival of the Jewish community of Budapest. The Jews had been in Hungary for more than a thousand years before the Nazis tried to wipe them out. Today only a small Jewish community remains. The prewar Hungarian Jewish population of 750 thousand is probably now down to about 75 thousand. Many were murdered, many fled, and many became refugees after the 1956 Hungarian revolution. The birthrate is low. And yet the Jewish community in Budapest remains the only significant one in eastern Europe.

The Jewish people, who brought heavy industry and banking skills to Hungary, still play an important

Opposite: Portrait of Raoul Wallenberg painted in 1944 by the Hungarian artist Stanislaw Dombrovszky and given to his mother in his memory.

58

part there. They contribute vitality, learning, and scholarship to literature, journalism, politics, and the various arts.

The Dohány Street Synagogue still stands in Budapest. Its garden contains almost 2,400 graves of those who were killed in 1945. There are also many memorial plaques. But Budapest also has reminders of the Jews' survival. Today, Hungarian Jews celebrate Yom Kippur without fear. Budapest also has the only rabbinical seminary in eastern Europe. Many of the chief rabbis of Prague, Warsaw, and even Moscow have been trained there. So, thanks in large part to Wallenberg, the Jewish community of Budapest has survived as a religious and spiritual powerhouse for all the countries of the Warsaw Pact.

Never forgotten

No one can ever forget that tens of thousands of Hungarian Jews survived only because of the incredible bravery of this one man — Raoul Wallenberg, the lost hero of the Holocaust.

We do not know what happened to Wallenberg during his cruel captivity in the years after he defied and defeated the Nazi death machine with nothing more than his courage and compassion. More than forty years after he disappeared, the mystery of Raoul Wallenberg's fate remains. Is the great man dead, as many believe? Or is he still alive as an old man in a Soviet prison camp — as is possible?

The campaign to find out the truth about Wallenberg continues to this day.

We may never know his fate. But one thing is certain. At a time when most of the world stood aside and did nothing, Raoul Wallenberg's rescue mission continues to stand out as one of the most extraordinary acts of the twentieth century.

Whether he is alive or dead, the example of his heroism and humanity will continue to provide a living inspiration to the whole world.

For More Information...

Organizations

The organizations listed below may provide you with more information about the Holocaust, the life of Raoul Wallenberg, and refugees and political prisoners in various countries. Many of these organizations are working to find out what really happened to Raoul Wallenberg and, if he is still alive, secure his release. Some publish newsletters that describe the work they are doing. When you write to them, be sure to tell them exactly what you would like to know, and remember to include your name, address, and age.

American Civil Liberties Union
132 West 43rd Street
New York, NY 10036

Amnesty International
322 Eighth Avenue
New York, NY 10001

Anne Frank Institute of Philadelphia
P.O. Box 2147
Philadelphia, PA 19103

Canadian Raoul Wallenberg Committee
P.O. Box 8040, Station F
Edmonton, Alberta
Canada   T6H 4N7

Free Wallenberg Committee
c/o Annette T. Lantos
1707 Longworth House Office Building
Washington, DC 20515

Raoul Wallenberg Committee
   of the United States
127 East 73rd Street
New York, NY 10021

Simon Wiesenthal Center
9760 West Pico Boulevard
Los Angeles, CA 90035

Books

The books listed below will help you learn more about Jewish customs and Jewish experiences during the Holocaust as well as about some of the individuals and countries involved in events of and surrounding the Holocaust. If these books are not in your local library or bookstore, ask someone there if they will order them for you.

About the Holocaust —

Clara's Story. Isaacman and Grossman (Jewish Publications Society)
The Diary of Anne Frank. Cadrain, adapter (Pendulum)
The Holocaust. Stein (Childrens Press)
The Holocaust: A History of Courage and Resistance. Stadtler (Behrman House)
My Brother's Keeper: The Holocaust Through the Eyes of an Artist.
   Bernbaum (Putnam)
Never to Forget: The Jews of the Holocaust. Meltzer (Harper and Row)
A Nightmare in History: The Holocaust. Chaikin (Ticknor and Fields)
Stolen Years. Zyskind (Lerner)
We Remember the Holocaust. Adler (Henry Holt and Co.)

About Jewish History, Customs, and Beliefs —

The Amazing Adventures of the Jewish People. Dimont (Behrman House)
I Am a Jew. Lawton (Franklin Watts)
Introduction to Jewish History. Rossel (Behrman House)
Way of the Jews. Jacobs (Dufour)
When a Jew Celebrates. Gersh (Behrman House)

About the Soviet Union and Hungary —

The KGB. Lawson (Wanderer)
The Land and the People of Hungary. Lengyel (Lippincott Junior)
The Soviet Union: The World's Largest Country. Gillies (Dillon)
Take a Trip to Hungary. Lye (Franklin Watts)

About World War II —

From Casablanca to Berlin. Bliven (Random House)
Invasion of Russia. Stein (Childrens Press)
Wartime Children, 1939 to 1945. Allen (Dufour)
World War II. Snyder (Franklin Watts)

Glossary

Allies
The nations that fought together against Germany, Italy, and Japan (the Axis countries) during World War II. They include the United States, Canada, Great Britain, France, the Soviet Union, and other countries.

Anti-Semitism
Prejudice, discrimination, hostility, or persecution aimed at Jewish people solely because they are Jewish, that is, because of their Jewish religion or background.

Architecture
The art and science of designing and overseeing the construction of buildings. Raoul Wallenberg came to the United States to study architecture.

Arrow Cross
Founded by Ferenc Szálasi, this was the Hungarian version of Germany's Nazi party. It was of little influence in Hungary until 1944.

Aryans
Originally the name given by historians to all descendants of the Indo-Europeans, the theoretical first race from which most West European cultures and languages came. Distorted by Hitler to mean people with "Nordic" coloring (that is, blond hair and blue eyes) who, he declared, were members of his "superior race."

Charisma
A personal quality that makes other people loyal and devoted to a leader with it.

Communist

A person who believes in a form of government, such as that found in the Soviet Union or China, in which ownership of private property is banned or kept to a minimum. In such a government, the needs of the nation as a whole are emphasized over individual or local needs.

Concentration Camps

Guarded prison camps in which people are detained for various reasons. These were first used by Spain during the Cuban rebellion of the 1890s.

Crematorium

A place with a furnace in which dead bodies are burned. If there are many such places, the word *crematoria* is used.

Death Camps

Camps established during World War II by the Nazis. Jewish civilians were kept in these camps until they were executed. In most cases the Jews did not realize that they were going to be killed. Among the most infamous death camps were Auschwitz, Buchenwald, and Dachau.

Death Marches

The forced marches of Jews from Budapest to Hungary's frontier — about 125 miles (200 km). Eichmann ordered this march in 1944, when Admiral Horthy ended the death trains leaving Hungary. Of the sixty thousand who left Budapest, at least ten thousand died on the marches. Most others died in Nazi death camps.

Deporting

Forcing a person or group of people to leave a country. During World War II, the Nazis deported Hungarian Jews from Hungary and sent them to the death camps in Poland.

Diplomats

Officials representing their own country while living in another country. Diplomats are charged by their government to work with the governments of whatever countries they are assigned to.

Embassy

The official residence and sometimes the offices of diplomats who are guests in another country.

Fascism (Fascist)

A general name for any movement (or person) with right-wing, nationalistic, pro-military, antidemocratic ideals. The original Fascists came from Italy and were led by Benito Mussolini.

"Final Solution"

The code name given by the Nazis to Hitler's ghoulish plan to kill all the Jews in Europe. The plan started in January 1942; the first victims died in March. By April

1945, more than six million Jews had died by gas or other means. Eichmann was high in the organization of men responsible for the plan.

Gestapo
The secret police of Nazi Germany; their name came from *Geheime Staatspolizei*, which means "secret state police."

Ghetto
A specific area of European cities where Jews were required to live. Some ghettos dated from the seventeenth century. This word has come to mean any heavily populated slum area where a poor minority group lives.

Gypsies
A wandering people scattered throughout the world and believed to have originated in India. They have their own language and culture and are known as musicians and fortunetellers. Gypsies accounted for one million of the twelve million people killed by the Germans before and during World War II.

Hitler, Adolf (1889-1945)
Born in Austria, he became leader of Germany's Nazi party. In 1923 he tried to overthrow the German government. While in prison for this, he wrote *Mein Kampf*, a rambling, poorly written book expressing his ideas of "Aryan" superiority and his hatred of Jews. He gained power in 1933 and became Germany's dictator that same year. By attacking Poland in 1939, he started World War II. He killed himself in Berlin in April 1945, rather than submit to capture by the Soviets.

Holocaust
The Jewish name for the period during World War II when Hitler was attempting to exterminate all the Jews of Europe. The word more generally means a great destruction or loss of life.

Jew
A member of the Jewish faith. Most Jews claim descent from the ancient Israelite nation of Palestine. Others have adopted Judaism as their faith.

Middle Ages
A loosely defined period, usually from about A.D. 900 to 1500, in the history of western Europe.

Nazi
A member of the National Socialist German Workers' Party, founded in 1919. In 1933, under Hitler, it seized power in Germany. All high officials in the Third Reich were Nazis.

Palestine
An area of land in the Middle East which has caused a great deal of political turmoil throughout history. The area roughly covers Israel and Jordan and parts of Lebanon and Egypt. It was the ancient homeland of the Jews.

Rabbi

The ordained head of a synagogue and a leader in the Jewish faith. The chief rabbi for an area holds a position somewhat like a Christian archbishop's.

Red Cross (and Red Crescent)

Founded in 1863 by Henry Dunant in Geneva, Switzerland, as a result of what he saw at the Battle of Solferino, in Italy. The International Red Cross and Red Crescent Movements cannot refuse to help someone in need because of that person's race, religion, or color.

Refugees

Persons who have been displaced from their home or country, usually for political or religious reasons.

Safe Houses

Houses claimed as part of the territory of Sweden so that German anti-Semitic laws did not apply in them. They were set up initially by Wallenberg and later by other embassies and the International Red Cross.

Scarlet Pimpernel, The

A well-known novel by Baroness Emmuska Orczy. Its plot concerns the rescuing of victims of the French Revolution in the 1790s by an upper-class Englishman.

Shoah

A Hebrew word meaning annihilation, it usually refers to the Holocaust.

Slav

Any member of the peoples of eastern Europe or Soviet Asia speaking a Slavonic-family language. The Nazis considered Slavs inferior to "Aryans." As a result, Soviet prisoners of war were treated far worse than British and French prisoners.

SS

From the initials of the *Schutzstaffel* (protection squad). Organized like a military group, they were the men who, among other things, acted as Hitler's bodyguards, concentration camp guards, and security forces.

Star of David

A six-pointed star that appears on the flag of Israel today. Used as a badge in yellow, it was the identifying mark for Jews in Nazi-controlled Europe.

Swastika

A cross with extensions at the ends of each leg of the cross. These extensions pointed in a clockwise direction. A symbol of the Nazi party, the swastika was a variation of the earlier symbol that represented good fortune among North American Indians.

Synagogue

A building where Jewish religious services are performed and religious instruction is given. The word comes from a Greek word that means "to bring together." It is also used to refer to a congregation of Jews gathered for worship or religious study and the organization of particular Jewish congregations.   Also spelled "synagog."

Third Reich
The Nazi government of Germany (1933-45). The First Reich was the Holy Roman Empire, regarded as the first major form of the German empire. The Second Reich (1871-1918) was the German empire resulting from the union of the independent German states into one country.

Yom Kippur
The Day of Atonement. This sacred day of the Jewish calendar is celebrated in late September or early October. It involves fasting and day-long prayers of penitence said in the synagogues.

Chronology

1912   **May** — Raoul Oscar Wallenberg dies of cancer, aged twenty-three.
August 4 — Raoul Gustaf Wallenberg (Raoul Oscar's son) is born in the Kapptsta Archipelago near Stockholm in Sweden.

1918   Raoul's mother marries Fredrik von Dardel.

1920   Following a Bolshevik uprising, Admiral Horthy takes power in Hungary. He blames Jews and urban communists for the uprising and executes many.

1923   Raoul travels alone by train to visit his grandfather, who was the Swedish ambassador to Turkey, in Istanbul. Raoul now has a younger half-brother and half-sister.

1931   After his compulsory military service, Raoul enrolls at the University of Michigan, Ann Arbor, to study architecture.

1933   **January 30** — Adolf Hitler becomes chancellor of the German Third Reich. Raoul spends the summer working at the Chicago World's Fair.

1935   Raoul returns to Sweden with a bachelor of arts degree with honors in architecture.
He wins second prize in an architecture competition in Stockholm.
He travels to Cape Town to train as a banker, and quickly decides banking is not the career he wishes to pursue.

1936   Raoul spends six months in Haifa (now in Israel), where he meets Jewish refugees from Germany.

1937   **March 21** — Raoul's grandfather dies.

1938   Raoul meets Koloman Lauer, a Hungarian Jew who runs an import/export business from Stockholm. He needs someone to run the foreign division. Raoul seems ideal.

1939   **September 3** — Great Britain and France declare war on Germany as a result of the invasion of Poland.

1941   **June 22** — Germany attacks the USSR, breaking an agreement in which they pledged not to wage war on each other.
August — The Hungarian army expels twenty thousand Jews into the Ukraine, then held by the Germans.
December — The United States declares war on the Axis powers (Germany, Italy, and Japan).

1942   **January 20** — General Heydrich outlines the "Final Solution" at the Wannsee Conference in Berlin.

1944   **January 22** — President Roosevelt of the United States sets up the War Refugee Board.
March 19 — The German occupation of Hungary begins.
May 14 — Mass deportations of Jews from the Hungarian provinces to the Auschwitz death camp begin.
June 23 — Wallenberg is recruited in Stockholm to try to save the Hungarian Jews from Eichmann. Over 116 thousand have already been shipped to Auschwitz.
He travels to Budapest via Berlin, where he visits his half-sister.
July 8 — Admiral Horthy signs an order ending the deportation of Jews.
July 9 — Raoul arrives in Budapest.
October 15 — Hungary asks the Allies for an armistice. The fascist Arrow Cross seizes power.
November 20 — The death marches to the Hungarian border begin. Over ten thousand people die on the 125-mile (200-km) journey.
December 8 — The siege of Budapest begins.
December 24 — Eichmann flees Budapest as the Soviets advance.
December 26 — Soviet troops surround Budapest.

1945   **January 17** — Raoul leaves for the Soviet Army headquarters at Debrecen with a military escort. He has not been seen by Westerners since.
Apparently he is taken directly to the Lubianka prison in Moscow. Then he disappears into the Gulag (Soviet prison camps).
The International and Central ghettos are liberated by Soviet troops.
March 8 — Soviet-controlled Hungarian radio announces that Raoul had been murdered on the way to Debrecen.
May 8 — VE (Victory in Europe) Day. Eichmann escapes the roundup of war criminals.
November 20 — War crimes trials begin in Nuremberg.

1947   **August 18** — The Soviet deputy foreign minister claims that "Wallenberg is not in the Soviet Union and is unknown to us."

1948 **April** — The Soviets confiscate the statue commissioned by the Jews of Budapest in memory of Wallenberg.
May 14 — The British mandate for Palestine ends. The Jews proclaim the State of Israel.

1958 **February 2** — Andrei Gromyko, then deputy foreign minister of the USSR, claims Wallenberg died in a Soviet prison on July 17, 1947.

1979 **February** — Raoul's mother and stepfather die within two days of each other. Shortly afterward, a tree is planted in the Avenue of the Righteous in Yad Vashem (the Israeli Holocaust memorial) in Jerusalem.

1981 Wallenberg is made an honorary citizen of the United States by Congress. By making him an honorary citizen, nations are able to exert pressure on the Soviet Union to account for Wallenberg's whereabouts.

1985 Raoul is made an honorary citizen of Canada.

1986 Raoul is made an honorary citizen of Israel.

Index